YOU DECIDE

My journey during a coma

by R.S. Guidolin

DEDICATION

To the medical team that, with persistence, acted in brilliant and inspiring ways to re-establish and stabilize my condition so I could live again.
And to my loving husband, children, grandchildren, family and friends that, with a deep love and devotion, elevated their prayers on my behalf.

ACKNOWLEDGMENTS

Acknowledgements to my editor, translator and publishing agent
Jonathan Valtriani de Carvalho

PREFACE

Voices were getting closer and closer... There were only a few steps left until she could be rescued...

No matter how hard I tried, my legs wouldn't respond and I couldn't even speak... Staggering, I leaned against the passage leading to the kitchen...

One step to the left was enough for them to see me...

In the meantime a commotion broke out and in a start; arms around my waist supported me....

Despite my obscured vision, I noticed myself being placed in the car and, an hour later, in a wheelchair, I was semi-consciously walking through the entrance hall of a hospital's Emergency Room.

At that time I had no idea that the hourglass of my life was spilling the remains of sand that pointed to my final moments...

LOOK AT ME

The final details for the long-awaited trip had been finalized; three days in Lisbon and then we would head to Italy and England. Visiting our children and getting the rest of our Italian documentation sorted would be our priority. This plan had been postponed on two other occasions due to the Coronavirus pandemic , which had ravaged the planet throughout 2020 and had not yet let up.

The sunny morning of Friday, September 17, 2021, emanated the scent of flowers from the woods and gardens, which, graced by the singing of birds, heralded a beautiful anticipation of spring.

While my husband and I waited for our visitors to arrive, we excitedly talked about our stay in Europe and England.

My brother-in-law and his wife were punctual. At 12 o'clock, as agreed, they were waiting at the gate of our house.

It had been a long time since we had seen them and we wanted to strengthen the relationship between our families.

After welcoming them and showing them our beautiful garden inside the house and other rooms, attracted by the aroma of the delicious roasted ribs that my husband had prepared, we headed to the kitchen.

A pleasant and lively conversation developed during the meal. Our families and the animals on my brother-in-law's farm were the main topics of discussion.

That reunion seemed perfect; until I felt a sudden uneasiness.

Without commenting on what was happening, I asked permission to leave and went to the bathroom.

The strong nausea I felt intensified, my legs became weak and everything around me began to spin...

Since no one would hear me to help myself, stumbling and on the verge of fainting, I held on to the walls. The path back to the kitchen seemed further due to how dizzy I felt. Finally, already leaning against the kitchen door frame, I took a step forward so that they could see me.

With a muffled voice I managed to mumble a few words... and then everything went dark. I held on to the sink until I sat on the floor.

In the blink of an eye, the harmonious gathering turned into a frantic rush, driven by intense concern on the part of my husband and our guests.

The couple quickly grabbed me and carried me, supported by their shoulders, to my husband who was already waiting in the car...

On the way to the hospital I regained consciousness for a few seconds when I heard my husband ask if I felt better. I could only look up at him and then I fainted again.

Hours later I was no longer in the comfort of my home, but huddled in a narrow space, similar to a gap between two floors.

Without having the slightest idea of what was happening, I was trapped in that cramped space, which was just over a meter high, from where I could see the ceiling extending close to my body and below me; below my knees, the uneven cement floor. A terrifying sensation of confinement amidst chills and suffocation began to torture me.

Hostage to that claustrophobic condition, an explosion of thoughts began to invade my mind. I imagined the worst possible tragedies that could have happened to me... Being the victim of a landslide, being kidnapped, buried alive, being run over, or any other tragic situation...

Devoid of any memories of the previous moments, almost dragging myself, I crawled in search of a way out.

- What's going on? – *I asked* .

Fear! So much fear! It would be insufficient to define such agony .

- How did I end up there?... And why? - *my thoughts, mixed with despair, accelerated.*

With effort I continued until I came across a thick pane of glass, which outlined a large rectangular window, through which I could not see clearly because it was fogged up.

Without knowing whether there was water on the other side, or whether my vision was blurred, I focused on that passage...

Consumed by anguish, after endless minutes, I managed to see a person moving in front... It was a male figure, who in continuous agitation, seemed to be waving.

Although his features stood out against the glass - because his face was hidden by a mask and large goggles - I imagined he was a diver.

- At last a hope gleamed. Something will be done to rescue me! - *that's what I thought.*

- Mrs. Rosicler ! Look at me! Mrs. Rosicler ! Look at me! – *exclaimed the man outside, in a loud voice .*

That emphatic and repetitive call, in the midst of other conversations, sounded strange... I didn't understand exactly what I should do, but it was clear that he was concerned about getting my attention, in order to divert my focus from despair and calm me down.

Despite the passage being blocked by the "glass obstacle" and the mask that covered his face, I could hear him clearly, which made me think that there was some equipment attached to the place where I was in the other space, which allowed communication.

I fixed my gaze in his direction and, due to the intense movement, I noticed the presence of other people who were moving around quickly in that environment.

I soon realized that the man was not submerged in a tank or pool, much less was he a diver as I had just imagined, but he was standing to my left and watching me attentively.

There were only a few minutes of this frenzy, until I could no longer see them and, at a speed beyond my comprehension, the claustrophobic sensation disappeared and I ended up somewhere else.

The fact that I had instantly moved to another location left me even more intrigued...

In fact, I didn't understand why I had been in that cubicle and then, without even moving or anyone guiding me, I ended up somewhere else.

This time the space was wide and the color white predominated from the floor to the curved wall to my left, which ended in a wide spiral ramp that extended to an upper floor. To my right and above there were no divisions, just an empty space, covered by a light-colored mist, which hid the existence of something beyond.

Free of worries, curiosity, or any feeling that generated doubt or discomfort; as if I knew where I should go, I advanced in narrow steps, towards the elevated part.

At first I heard tumultuous conversations, but I couldn't see the people interacting. Without understanding what they were saying or where the voices were coming from, I remained interested in what I was experiencing until the external sounds silenced.

As I continued, someone joined me; it was a young man. Although I didn't see where he had come from, I wasn't afraid, because at first I imagined he was one of my sons. I didn't see his face clearly, but I remember that his hair was dark and he was about the same height as me. I thought he was one of my sons, because he showed that he knew me very well.

With a calm gesture and special attention, he handed me something that resembled a control used to access computer games, but larger, or at least that was the comparison that came to mind. There were several elements similar to cubes inserted into that strange rectangular object.

In an unusual way, as if in the blink of an eye, my mind became conditioned to the young man's, as if we were talking in thought. At that moment my understanding expanded, I could understand that the purpose of the device would be to control the opening or closing of that place... Then he explained to me that it should close in stages. I understood that he was referring to a passage, or to the environment itself. He warned me not to close it completely, to leave a part open, and that I should pay attention to the time.

I didn't know exactly how the process would occur, or I don't remember it being explained, but I followed the instructions skillfully.

Amazed at what I had been able to do, I continued down that ramp, focused on what had guided me, until I reached the second floor. On this floor, in the central part, there was a large rounded opening. I only had time to look down through that wide gap and the entire space around me began to diminish, as if it were shrinking. The person accompanying me warned me that I should hurry.

I tried to be quick in activating that "device" due to the shrinking phenomenon that occurred in the form of a gigantic curved chinese fan, which produced a sound similar to cracking, until a smaller passage was left half-open.

Despite understanding what was supposed to be done, I didn't get any answer about what had happened or why.

A mixture of curiosity and concern started to bother me again:

-*"Where am I?... What's happening?... Why am I here?" –
I continued to ask questions.*

Being in that exotic place sparked my interest, as did the impression that, in that short space of time, I had evolved significantly in my understanding of various aspects, especially regarding my existence.

As everything, until then, happened in an accelerated process, I did not enjoy this experience for long, because they called me again:

- Mrs. Rosicler ! Mrs. Rosicler ! Look at me!... – *insisted , a male voice, as before.*

- Why look? – *I thought , intrigued* – Even so, I complied with the request.

I opened my eyes and slowly moved my head to the left. With my blurred vision I saw a man wearing a white lab coat, positioned next to a wide, tall metal rod. His rounded face behind a mask and the tuft of dark hair that came down from the cap, exposed on his forehead and his large glasses, did not provide a complete description of who he could be, but, on the other hand, the restlessness of other people in the room demonstrated that the situation was tense.

From that moment on, in the midst of all that commotion, I realized that I was in a hospital. And that the man I had previously imagined to be a diver was actually a doctor, who this time told me not to be afraid, to stay calm, that they were there with me...

As I did not feel any pain or physical discomfort, I hardly knew that I had come back from a second cardiorespiratory arrest, and that in the period between successive resuscitations I was not immersed in a trance, hallucinating, or even dreaming.

Rather, I had been literally " teleported ", if I may put it that way, as there was no other logic to such displacements.

These transpositions did not include matter, or rather, my physical state or my body. They occurred as if I were snapping my fingers, or simply passing through a door, as quickly as if there were no obstacles, not even great distances. They were comings and goings that happened spontaneously, no one provoked them, or at least did not perceive any external action.

When my heart started beating again, it was as if a "portal", or the passage to where it had been, closed quickly.

In this way, at the same speed that I passed to some "other side", I returned to my body in the hospital bed.

Despite having seen, even if only briefly, the commitment of the medical team, the idea that I had died had not yet occurred to me, but at the same time I was aware that my situation was not at all good.

As for the cracks I heard while I was looking through the open gap, I assume they could have been from a defibrillator trying to revive me.

I stayed with that team for a considerable amount of time, until I left again, as fast as lightning...

A NEW OPPORTUNITY

This time I didn't see myself trapped, nor did I find myself in a flowery garden, or in the middle of green fields, nor did I even see fog or a tunnel of light...

Another "dimension" appeared before my eyes... unlike any place I had ever seen, where the vibrant reddish color shone from fully illuminated, concave-looking walls.

Where there were no points or beams of light that could identify lamps or luminaires...

Still without answers for those intriguing "journeys" in which I had not used any means of transport and without any clear pattern of what was happening, I stood for a while in front of that gigantic dome.

Its structure, despite its artificial appearance, seemed not to have been built with bricks, cement, or any other element that he knew, as it resembled a single colored crystal, carved to perfection, without cracks or joints...

I glimpsed that luminous expanse without being able to see where it began or ended... I looked to the sides and up and felt very small in the face of that immensity, which was also exceedingly deep.

The reddish light, with a soft burgundy tone, was intense; I could see it with a clarity beyond my capacity. There was no white light, or any other color besides burgundy, in that place.

The luminosity was reflected through large hexagonal pieces, seamlessly, with a faint transparency, which resembled rubies embedded in the walls. At least that was the definition I gave to that shape and strong brightness, whose splendor I had never witnessed.

On this occasion I didn't have "control" in my hands, so I imagined that the previous space had been completely opened, or was its extension.

I heard voices echoing again, coming from outside, or from the hospital environment. A child's voice stood out, asking someone to play with her. I could see the image of a woman and the child reflected high up on the bright wall to my right, both looking attentively and excitedly at a laptop.

The initial feeling was of being very close to the other patients in the hospital and the medical team, as if there was only a space separating us.

But, little by little I distanced myself and the confused conversations stopped....

Ecstatic, I continued to observe the surroundings with greater interest. It was surreal. Not even the most beautiful and elaborate cinematic environment, mimicking the grandeur and beauty of the universe, could be compared to what I witnessed.

Despite being a bit apprehensive, the serenity and welcoming atmosphere of that place gave me a feeling of lightness, as if I were floating...

Everything was so perfect that my youthfulness had blossomed. It was as if there were no more problems or fears.

I was wearing a simple dress, without any adornments or other details, in a pearly color, which flared out gently below the waist and left my ankles exposed.

As the space narrowed and the light dimmed, peace and an inexplicable feeling of well-being compelled me to move forward.

At a certain point I was interrupted.... A female voice stopped me.

In a subtle but emphatic way, a woman warned me:

- No! Don't go! – *he said in a somewhat pleading tone* .

- If you continue you will never come back! – *she warned*

Although this warning did not match what was being presented to me, I stopped for a moment and paid attention to where the voice was coming from.

There was a brief pause.

- You decide! – *she added* .

I don't remember the woman's appearance, or even if she said anything else; my mind only pictured a figure. However, the reality I was experiencing made it clear that I had not heard the sound emitted by my own voice in my subconscious, much less was I dreaming.

A complex situation. On the one hand, what she had told me made it clear that there were only two possibilities:

Follow that attractive path, or return to the uncertainties and challenges that awaited me...

As much as I felt comforted and free from regrets on that new path, I wanted to go back. I felt like I needed to do something more... and one of the reasons would be to take care of my husband and children, even though they were adults; among other relevant things, which I don't remember.

I imagine that anyone else in my place would have wanted to continue, because the feeling of being completely free from futile things and material goods produced endless peace.

So much so that I no longer felt included in my daily life, I didn't even remember what had been left behind, in fact; in the condition I found myself in, there were no more worries or anything that would disturb that incredible feeling of well-being.

I had the strong impression of having stayed a long time in this splendid place and interacting with other people.

After my decision, I heard a faint voice, like that of a girl:

- Stay close to the tree ! – *she admonished me with a firm and prolonged intonation , as if she were intoning a warning* .

At that moment, which connoted more of a farewell, I did not pay attention to the meaning or symbolism of this enigmatic orientation. However, I understood its importance.

Since there were no barriers between time and space, I began to hear; instead of a soft voice, screams, which erupted in a tone of despair.

- MRS ROSICLER! MRS ROSICLER! MRS ROSICLER! LOOK AT ME! LOOK AT ME! ... DON'T STOP LOOKING!... DON'T STOP LOOKING AT ME!...

- What is this? What happened? - I asked *myself, scared* .

I saw a doctor next to me again.

He probably had to shout because of my distracted gaze. It was the technique he used to keep me focused and not faint.

I fixed my attention on those dark brown eyes, which stared at me wide open.

Still without having the slightest idea that I had died again after sixteen minutes of resuscitation, by divine providence and the persistence of the medical team, I came back from this third and long cardiorespiratory arrest.

The unfinished periods, in which I found myself under a slab and in other places, occurred in the interval of time in which they were proceeding with the resuscitations.

I felt confused because I didn't know why I was involved in this process, in which I was going to unknown places, as if I was wandering, still without a destination...

After these circumstances, I began to see myself, more than once, in other places, which were not at all pleasant, and which resembled an excavation in the raw earth, like a tunnel or cave.

These tunnels were different from the space below the ground where they had been, as they were higher, with a wide column of earth in the central part, as if it were a poorly carved pillar, or support column , which marked out a circumference around it.

The first time I was in this "cave," I felt as if I were inside a plastic bag, or in an enormous "placenta," which could fit my body, shrunken like that of a fetus. I imagined myself in a second pregnancy, but a very troubled one, in which I had been subjected to unfavorable conditions in which I was unable to defend myself, as probably happens with a baby with malformations, or when unwanted.

This "large package" appeared to be attached to something on the ceiling or wall and moved slowly and steadily around the pillar.

Anguished and unable to react, I couldn't think of anything else other than escaping from there, or for someone to take me out of that dark place...

While "the placenta", "or envelope" seemed to move, giving the impression of rotating "through the narrow tunnel", a sound, not so shrill, like that of a machine resonating uninterruptedly and in rhythms.

For a moment I thought I heard my husband speaking in another room, or noticed his presence, as I imagined I was confined below the sidewalk at the back of my house, near the kitchen.

Then I heard drums beating, which sounded like rituals. I could see the people there. A man dressed in white clothes, crouched low to the ground, moved quickly in a circle and dragged some object or branches and said words whose meaning I did not understand, but it was as if he was calling for someone.

Each lap around that "dirt hole" became more and more distressing... to the point where I begged, even in my mind, for them to take me out of that place.

I wanted to scream... However, I was aware that I wouldn't be able to...

At that time, a warm liquid began to rise, as if it were coming from my legs.

When the water reached my throat, I felt like I was about to drown...

It was all so real that I literally started to suffocate.

– I'm going to die! I'm going to die! – *I despaired* . – Someone come save me! – *I cried out in my subconscious* .

I thought it was the end for me, because I knew there was no one around to understand what was happening to me.

I remember that the sound continued, but louder and this time prolonged, in this way: " Piiiiiiiiiiiiiiiiiiiiiiiiiiiiiiii .... "

Because I was being "projected" from one place to another, I started to think that all these events were just nightmares; that I would soon wake up and everything would be fine and my life would return to normal.

Big mistake, the reality was different.

It wasn't a dream and I wasn't in a cave, but rather in a room in the Intensive Care Unit, connected to several devices that, attached to the wall, gave me the sensation of spinning and being inside a package.

In this interspersed series of dizzying sensations, sometimes I saw myself in a cave and other times in the ICU, but it was the same place, which was portrayed by my subconscious as a disastrous place, due to the loneliness, uncertainties and fears, which produced the idea of being inside of a tunnel.

The movement I felt could have been dizziness, due to the intense discomfort.

Due to this latest fatality, my condition changed, like a flash of lightning I left "the cave" (ICU) and ended up in the living room of my house.

In extreme weakness, with the impression that an immense weight was pressing down on my body... unable to even move my arms and legs, sitting on the largest red suede sofa in the spacious living room, I partially raised my eyelids with effort... Hexagonal figures filled my field of vision, as if I were looking through a beehive, the grayish color prevailed and covered the entire environment, like a fog.

My husband was sitting next to the bathroom, on the smaller sofa to my left. His fallen expression showed the deepest sadness... Although I didn't fully understand what was happening and why he was so desolate, I remained there, sitting, without the desire or strength to try to communicate, just observing him...

After opening my eyes fully, the room, darkened by dusk, instantly lit up, without the lights even being turned on.

In this interesting experience, I first saw the darkness of the room and then the light, which highlighted the environment with vibrant colors.

For a moment, I had the strange sensation that light was reflected from my gaze.

In fact, only I could see that light, as my husband couldn't even see me and remained under the dim lighting of a few lamps.

Without understanding the magnitude of what had happened, I began to be careful not to keep my eyes open, because in my limited understanding I feared that the intense light would disturb my husband, who seemed sleepy.

This unusual condition lasted until I was revived again, because the water I felt rising was real, and had lodged in my lungs, causing yet another cardiorespiratory arrest.

BY A THREAD

One day, the presence of a doctor caught my attention. She appeared to be under 50 years old, was blonde, had straight hair that fell to her shoulders, had fair skin and a rather large figure. At first, she seemed like a good-natured person.

During one of her visits, I obtained information about her: "that she sometimes came to work by motorcycle, that she was going through a divorce and that she had two children, a 10-year-old boy and a 17- or 18-year-old daughter who was studying to be a nurse, among other facts about her personal life." Knowing about her private life didn't seem useful to me at all, but I found out about it somehow. Perhaps because I had overheard a conversation next to me.

That day, when I was observing her more closely, I heard her speak; however, the impression was that I understood, or read her thoughts:

- It would be better for me to die than for someone else to die. I should have no better chance of surviving.

Maybe I thought this way because of my age; 56 years old... I wasn't young and my clinical condition was one of the worst, or I simply already considered myself dead...

Later I saw the same doctor talking to a young man. They were positioned close to the door of my room, I wasn't sure if it was a resident doctor or a nurse who was accompanying her.

It may seem strange to refer to the episodes in this way, but I cannot explain how I saw them moving around the room and in other environments, if I was in a coma, with my eyes closed and my body completely paralyzed.

On the other hand, the fact that I was moving around the room and observing the movement around me did not require any explanation for me. It was as if I had come to fully understand the "two versions" of my existence.

I was very close to them, standing, and inexplicably I could hear even the sighs they made and decipher their thoughts.

For a moment I looked to my left and was confronted with my deplorable condition; lying face down, with the head of the bed raised and a tube coming out of my mouth. Despite being moved, I didn't question why I could see my body, and even more so in that state...

On this occasion, the most terrifying thing was hearing what the two were talking about.

The doctor said that she would turn off my oxygen and/or put some "medicine" in the oxygen. I didn't understand exactly what the procedure would be, I just knew that my fears flared up and intensified my desire to run away from there.

It wasn't long before the doctor, with long strides, walked towards my bed. Her heavy breathing, unsteady gait and apprehensive expression betrayed her fears.

She positioned herself to my right, facing the machines that kept me alive, raised her arm and proceeded with some alteration.

At that very moment I felt a desperate suffocation.

I had the useless urge to scream for help again...

I didn't understand why they did that. Maybe they really thought I was dead, or because it was a hospital with limited resources, they needed the respirator for another patient with a better chance of survival, as had happened a few months ago at the height of the Coronavirus pandemic . I find this somewhat understandable, since some hospitals did not have equipment for all the patients in serious condition, and there were still many infected people who needed to be intubated.

At first the sensation was similar to when you hold your breath during a deep dive and are unable to come to the surface.

Because I couldn't breathe and felt my final moments, endless anguish took over every fiber of my body.

My senses began to grow hazy...the last breaths slowly faded away...

Finally the oxygenation stopped completely.

The thin thread that held my life together had been broken...

- It's all over for me! - *I asked , in my suffocated despair* .

The doctor was quick and soon left the room.

- I was left alone! Abandoned to my own fate!

This time no alarm sounded for anyone to come and help me, at least I didn't hear any sound.

The few chances of survival had literally been blocked.

I was now definitely leaving... the "comings and goings" between cardiorespiratory arrests and the heartbeat would cease completely...

As a spectator of the transition process to a new journey, I watched my life being cut short... Without goodbyes... Without the affection of a loved one to hold my hand and tell me they loved me... Without the right to defense, without leaving any traces...

No one would know what had happened to me, nor about my fierce battle for life, besides the fact that my brain had been in perfect activity the whole time...

It was in this last moment... in the final moment of my consciousness, that I realized that I was not alone and much less abandoned as I had imagined.

After the doctor left; something simply unbelievable happened...

I saw a man walking towards my bed, his clothes were white, different from most health professionals, who wore light green lab coats.

I couldn't see his face clearly or where he had come from; because besides my body being weak, my vision was blurred, even so I noticed that he wasn't in a hurry or hasty.

He calmly stood in front of the equipment and made a new change.

Little by little the air returned... I took a breath and felt the oxygen flow into my lungs and my breathing normalized.

Although it was not clear who had adjusted the respirator and made the oxygenation normal; whether it was the boy the doctor had spoken to, or someone else; a warm feeling of relief and gratitude replaced the fear of those fateful minutes that seemed like desperate hours.

With this experience I understood that when my organs were stabilized, I, or rather my spirit, "circulated" through the environments, in a "floating walk", without impact on the ground and when cardiorespiratory arrests occurred, or some invasive procedure, I returned to my body after resuscitation.

This happened five times, during which the resurrections provided the "reconnection" of my spirit to my body.

IN ABSOLUTE DEPENDENCE

Faced with this disastrous episode, my main objective remained to escape from the hospital from that moment on, as quickly as possible.

Like a speeding computer, my brain worked non-stop, this time immersed in escape plans.

By seeing what was happening around me, I got some information:

The bed I was in was kept elevated. I also knew that to my left there was a large window with wide panes of glass that were usually left open. I even saw the curtain sway in the wind and a woman, perhaps a nurse, pointing outside. That day I imagined that she was showing me a way out through the window, because I would certainly have been blocked by the nursing staff working in the room next to my room.

It didn't take me long to realize that my plans were of no use to me, that they were foolish on my part, because I couldn't even move my eyelids.

I found myself at the mercy of fate... and to make matters worse I was on the top floor of that building.

There was no longer any doubt for me that my clinical condition was extremely serious and that what I was experiencing were not fantasies, but rather the planned reality between the period of time of each resuscitation through the cardioverter and other procedures.

Subject to so much tension, there were few conversations around me that made me feel good, like the day when a doctor, or nurse, I'm not sure, spoke to a woman about his religion and invited her to visit his religious community.

Because the subject sparked my interest, I paid attention to what they were talking about.

He commented on a recent conference or service he had attended, which had helped him gain new perspectives.

In a way, this conversation helped me relax and ease my distress.

At another time, two nurses who were caring for me were talking about a course that one of them was taking and that was proving very useful to her.

The other day the subject was not at all edifying:

- Do you know the man in the room next door? - *said the nurse* - He's dead! - *she replied in a muffled voice* .

No other thought came to mind other than that I could be next... Which made me even more worried.

At another moment I heard them say again:

- You know that patient? – *said the nurse, even mentioning his name* – He passed away too!

I wasn't upset that they talked naturally about these unpleasant subjects, because I knew they didn't even imagine that I was listening to them, much less seeing them.

In another situation, I found myself on a moving stretcher, nurses were following a ramp with curves and a steep slope, from where I could see the door of an elevator opening - I felt like I was sitting on the stretcher and watching the entire journey - I was removed quickly. I don't know where they were taking me, but I remember feeling embarrassed for wearing only a gown.

Despite receiving a lot of daily care, I once felt uncomfortable hearing a nurse's voice. He was rude, made disturbing laughs and spoke loudly.

I caught a glimpse of him entering the room.

I knew he had come to "tap" me on the back.

- Again! I can't take this beating on my back anymore! - *I muttered in my mind, when he approached.*

The nurse slapped me so hard that my body seemed to shudder with each slap. I felt no pain, but the discomfort was extreme, as if waves or tremors were forming over me, similar to a cramp that radiated throughout my body.

I remembered other "slapping" sessions that bothered me.

I later learned that the purpose of this maneuver was to help clear the obstruction in my lungs, which had filled with water twice.

On this day, this professional came accompanied by a colleague, who seemed to be more withdrawn.

As he continued with the "tapotagem ", he spoke uninterruptedly, while the other remained silent.

Among so many trivial and baseless subjects, at one point he began to utter obscene words, which caused me extreme indignation:

- Aren't you ashamed to say all this in my presence? - *I thought , with disgust.*

I still can't explain exactly how these perceptions of mine manifested themselves, but I also saw the nurse who was with the indecent companion, positioned on the opposite side. He looked like my son Marcelo, only he was bald and thinner.

As if I understood his thoughts, I was able to learn a little about his character. He was more thoughtful and balanced and disagreed with his colleague's behavior.

Between one event and another, I continued to hear movement around me, and I even saw the faces of some people.

Since I had never opened my eyes at any point, as I was in a deep coma, "my other self", which I recognize as my spirit, was watching and, in a certain way, interacting with much of what was happening.

Everything happened as if I were simply changing clothes; one moment I was physically in bed, dependent on the functioning of the machines, the next I was out of my body observing places and people. In this new "clothing", which was not tangible, I felt as if I were on alert, as the guardian of my body, and I could not leave or distance myself from the ICU room for a long time.

In another circumstance I felt trapped in a bag again, but the place, represented by my mind, this time was not a tunnel and was also different from the room I was in. It was a wide, open space with a wide, steep oval staircase, as if forming a large half-moon, and stretching out in front. I felt like I was on a stage with raised bleachers all around, however the place seemed abandoned, due to its precarious structure. From this place I watched my husband approach, stay by my side for a few minutes and then leave accompanied by a young man.

I felt like I had interacted with him, but I was sad that he had only spent so little time with me and that he didn't take me home.

After that I saw him near some people who were entering a beautiful building, which looked like a Temple to me, he just watched from afar and didn't go in.

Despite the intense desire to escape, to flee from where I was, I was aware that I could not leave, or be absent for even a minute from that "bag" or "bubble", it would be the end for me, because I knew that I would not survive outside of it.

In fact, the "bubble" in which I imagined myself was the representation reproduced by my subconscious of the devices that, with their wires, needles and hoses, "like a dome", connected to my body and sustained my life.

CONNECTING THE FACTS

In another episode, I saw my husband Ozair, accompanied by a couple of our friends, waiting in a hospital waiting room. I imagined that they had come to visit me.

Even in the darkness that enhanced the nocturnal aspect of the environment, I could see them at a short distance, despite being in my bed. It was as if my vision surpassed barriers, projected itself through walls and other obstacles and reached them.

In this supernatural condition, I saw them and also heard them talking.

My friend Rosangela said she was sorry that visitors were not allowed at the hospital. Among other random things, my husband mentioned that he no longer ordered pizzas because I couldn't eat them, as I am diabetic and very careful about my dietary restrictions, and he didn't want me to feel like I was craving them.

Afterwards I heard one of them say a prayer, however, the words used were different from usual, which I do not remember.

I then heard my husband say that if I died he wouldn't have the courage to get dressed, so he asked my friend to, when necessary, take a white outfit from the closet and dress me.

I was extremely indignant when I heard him speak in this way, because I felt very alive... in fact: more than alive! At that exact moment I no longer felt like I was in the hospital bed, but standing very close to him, in the kitchen of our house.

- He thinks I'm going to die! Why? Why? ... - *I retorted impatiently, as I looked at him* .

I then noticed my son Juliano talking to his friend. They were near a car, both holding their guitars, playing and singing with their beautiful voices. I imagined that they were outside the hospital, in a courtyard.

At one point Juliano said:

- How about this song? – *he sang a part* .

The friend replied that he didn't know the lyrics.

It sounded like an Italian song to me.

My son told him that he wanted to sing for me.

At the same moment I heard her melodious voice resound in a beautiful song and slide softly through the window into my room in the hospital.

Overcome with emotion, I felt an extra strength and a renewing joy invade my soul, for having been intoned in this majestic form of love.

The voice and expressions of our friends, Ozair and Juliano, were clear, so real that they seemed to be present, as if they were in front of me.

My hearing and vision were much sharper, I could hear them and see them clearly, for this reason I assumed they were waiting in some reception to visit me, but at the same time I was aware that they would not be authorized to do it.

After hearing the song and part of their conversation, a loud sound erupted, it was from the devices that stabilized the functioning of my organs, which with a shrill sound, like an alarm, in a loud and rapid sequence, emitted an alert.

Amidst the bang, I felt as if I had suddenly woken up and opened my eyes.

Someone ran into the room, but I have no memory of what happened after all this commotion.

On the next occasion I saw my son Juliano again, this time standing in the hallway of our dining room, positioned next to the long table where we gathered for special family events. I saw him from a higher plane, as if a "rounded window" had been opened, "tearing the air itself", next to the large oil painting that we have in the center of the living room wall.

His physiognomy and gestures expressed a certain discontent. I could not discern whether he was speaking or thinking, because my perception, for both situations, was the same:

- Dad always has that story! I'm not going out there! - he *grumbled , restless* .

While one of my daughters waited in the courtyard outside of the house to be invited in, Juliano saw his father upset with her presence, due to past intrigues.

At another time, perhaps on the same day, I found myself outside my house, below the sidewalk. It was as if there was a cave between the house and the garden. I felt like I was standing. I looked up and saw some of my children gathered together: Luciana and her children, William, Juliano, Priscila and her children, Marcelo, Ozair Neto and Ozair , my husband. The faces of each one were clear.

Everyone was talking excitedly and socializing, I could see that there was a celebration among them.

And there I was: outside, "under the ground", in extreme physical weakness, unable to be with them – or so I imagined .

- Why am I not with them? Why can't I get out of here? - I *struggled to walk and whined.*

I also asked why they had "imprisoned" me, because that was how I felt: a prisoner.

The impression was that I was standing, with hands tied, one on each side, to metal rods. I tried to move my legs, but I couldn't... I had no strength, and my body felt like it had tripled in weight.

I was intrigued by these children whom I could see from our house. Shouldn't they be in England? and my eldest daughter in Campinas, São Paulo where they lived?

- What are you doing here at home? – *I asked* .

Still without answers, I still had an intense desire to understand exactly what was going on, because when I found myself outside the hospital, my understanding of what was happening was very limited.

It had become distressing to see and hear people and no one to see me or interact with me.

Then my son William accompanied me, entering silently and with his head down to the place where I was, in that same "basement" below the sidewalk of the house, close to the living room. In this way I still visualized the hospital room; as if it were a cold and sad tunnel, where I had been "imprisoned".

William looked scared and Marcelo followed right behind, Ozair was close to them and instructed them to look at me from a distance.

I felt as if I were sitting on the bed and following them with my eyes. I could see their faces clearly.

William looked at me from a distance, his face immersed in deep sorrow and carrying the fear of my departure.

I was distressed that they only looked at me and didn't even talk to me, didn't even come closer and, what's more, left within a few minutes.

I wanted to go with them, to leave that dark place, but they left me there, alone... - That's what I thought.

- Why can't I go home??? – *I lamented again.*

I caught a glimpse of my daughter Priscila outside the hospital, next to a car. She was very upset that her two young children were not allowed to come in to see me. I remember her complaining to someone about this restriction; I heard her insinuate that if she paid a fee they would let the children in.

She ended up coming to see me alone.

Since the doctors gave no hope that I would live, they allowed some of my children, those who lived further away and my husband, to see me to say goodbye for the last time.

The fact that I was having "out of body experiences with heightened vision and hearing," allowed me to be in their presence in some way, even if I didn't fully know how this displacement proceeded.

Later on, I witnessed a common situation involving the family of my son Marcos, who lived near my house.

My daughter-in-law, sitting on a bench with her little son on her lap, and his stepdaughter were talking. It was a family matter, where the stepdaughter said she was going to the beach, or on a trip to spend the night... I heard my son say he intended to visit me.

I even thought they were in the hospital next to me, because this time it was as if I was watching them while sitting on my bed. It didn't take long for me to realize that my body was still motionless and I could only see and hear them. Even though I tried hard, I couldn't move my body to get closer to them, I just watched them without interacting, and that was what happened every time I saw my family.

I realized that I maintained a greater connection with family members and others who tuned in with their thoughts to desire my well-being more intensely.

It is interesting that there was no division of time or distance for everything that happened, it was a sequence of facts and places; one moment connected to the other.

The weakness and discomfort were constant and intense in almost all circumstances, except when I was in two places that differed in every aspect from the normality of my life, where I could walk and feel free from sorrows and any discomfort. In other places I felt weak, I could barely see the surroundings and people, however, I remained inert.

GAS CHAMBER

Since there was no distance for me to cover, this time I found myself inside a huge warehouse, with a very high ceiling; it seemed to be an abandoned place. In the center of the warehouse there was something that looked like a huge cage, or a wire dome. Police officers, I think there were more than three, were escorting some young men, around 10 to 15 of them. Their appearance, their thinness and the fact that they were dressed in rags, with their hands tied behind their backs, showed that they were subjugated.

I watched the police officers open the glass dome with their own hands, lifting it up, and then they let the boys in.

Inside the place there were chairs lined up and each group was forced to enter and sit down. After everyone was tied to the chairs, I sat behind them, in the last row, and only then did they close that " big cage ".

The pitiful situation of those boys connoted a life without rules and without direction, which had led them to that disastrous future.

In a few seconds I saw, one by one, their heads hanging forward, after fainting.

It didn't take long for them to open the dome.

A deadly gas had been released and those men had been killed by poisoning.

For fear of suffocating, I held my breath for a while, but without understanding why the gas hadn't hurt me, I followed the second group, as no one seemed to care about my presence.

At the same time that I witnessed that massacre, I was aware that no matter how much I wanted to, I would not be able to interfere.

Then another uniformed man, who appeared to be superior to the others, entered through a wide double-leaf door. This military man seemed to be exuding anger, shouted at his subordinates for a few seconds and then hurriedly left. I did not understand the reason for such aggression, but his demeaned posture and harsh words showed his disapproval.

I had never been to that place and I don't know why I participated, even if only as an observer, in that sad outcome.

What I felt on that occasion was not only deep regret and indignation at that scene, but empathy for those young-looking men.

Even if these were individuals who lived on the fringes of society, I thought that there could have been a whole life story with its problems, as a backdrop, in which preventive measures, while they were teenagers, could have helped to reverse, if not alleviate the degree of dependence, whatever it was, chemical, psychological... before it culminated in that inhumane and tragic end.

From there, in the blink of an eye, I found myself on the upper floor of my house, above my bedroom, where there was only an abandoned attic. I felt as if I were in a box seat and through a large window, I began to observe the central part of my house, from where I saw my husband. Everything seemed different, instead of the beautiful and welcoming winter garden; a spacious hall with a well-designed staircase, which widened at the foot, outlined by careful handrails, occupied the new space.

The new layout of the house did not catch my attention, however, the sadness that my husband showed moved me. Sitting at the foot of the stairs, with a dismayed expression, he caressed one of my dresses, exposed over his legs.

This time, the same rectangular object from the other occasion was in my hands. I don't remember anyone handing me the device. At that time, I felt familiar with that "equipment" and understood that I was being able to monitor something. I don't remember if it was related to "time", "location" or some other situation, as had happened previously.

As I looked at my husband, a slender, dark-haired young woman with a frightened expression sat behind me, paying attention to what I was doing. It was as if she wanted to learn how to use the device and also didn't know what was happening to her or why she was there.

This situation gave me the feeling of being a participant of some kind of test or a learning process where I was in an immersion of knowledge destined for a future occasion, of which I had no knowledge about.

SOLEMN MOMENT

I didn't know some of the places I was present at, as it happened in this episode: I was in a large courtyard and watched a ceremony being organized.

Many people in sumptuous attire crowded into this spacious place, surrounded by walls. Many of them were wearing military uniforms and were chatting enthusiastically.

Sitting in a wheelchair, unable to move a single finger and not understanding why I was participating in yet another event, I remained attentive to everything that was happening.

Shortly before the ceremony began, a light-skinned gentleman of medium height approached and placed a cape, similar to a royal blue wool poncho , over my shoulders and pinned a rounded brooch with carved details between the flaps of the shawl.

His attitude was as if he was paying homage to me, which gave me the feeling of being safe and, in a way, protected.

I don't remember how the ceremony went, but I know it lasted until almost dusk, when everyone left and a large steel gate was closed .

- Why did they leave me there, alone...unable to move...? - *I asked, desolate, when I was left behind .*

I felt deep sadness that my presence had been ignored and I had no idea how I could get out of that place, with no one to help me.

It didn't take me long to realize that those people hadn't seen me, except for the man who had pinned the brooch.

While I was quickly looking around to locate someone, I saw my daughter Eloise and her two children, who despite being an ocean away, as they live in the western United States, I could see them through the gate, as if they were on the other side of the wall.

A middle-aged man accompanied her. I heard her comment to him that she really wanted to see me.

I watched her from afar, until she left with her head down, as she hadn't been able to be with me.

Just before dark , the gate opened again; a gentleman, somewhat bald on the top of his head, who appeared to be about 50 years old, no more than 1.75 m tall, and with a face that reminded me of my father, entered the courtyard with quick steps and walked towards me. He seemed to be the same kind gentleman who had placed the poncho over my shoulders and the brooch. I noticed that he could see me, however, without saying a word, he gave a discreet smile and started building a fire in front of me and then lighting it.

Men and women, with torn clothes, began to come in quickly. They passed close to my chair, but without looking at me, because I believe they did not see me.

After positioning themselves around the fire, they began to sing a song and dance, which made the women's long, simple dresses sway with their movement. Although the melody was out of tune, the enthusiasm with which they sang made the rhythm cheerful and contagious. The lyrics were in Italian and said in translation: *"We are poor Italians, yes, poor Italians, but very happy... very happy... "siamo poveri italiani, si, ... poveri italiani, ma molto felici... molto felici..."* They repeated this chorus with excitement.

Even though the occasion violated the protocols of distance and time period; due to the language and the old clothes they wore, I knew that I was in Italy and that those humble people did not have a roof over their heads and were used to coming to that place due to the harsh winter.

Despite feeling a strong connection with these impoverished Italians, none of them seemed familiar to me except for the man who lit the fire.

The simplicity of this new setting was a stark contrast to the rich participants in the previous civic-military event.

THE UNEXPLAINABLE

On the next occasion, I observed my husband at a religious meeting held in a shed at a friend's house. I heard him speak with his strong and vibrant intonation, which held the attention of the participants.

I followed all the movement from a distance, but I felt like I was below ground. This time, I was in the water and surrounded by floating plants, and, like the other times, I wanted to be present.

On this occasion I noticed that a child, a boy no more than 4 years old, could see me through a crack in the floor and tried to tell the others what he saw, but they paid no attention to him.

Because there is no sense, meaning, or even division of time, I did not detail one episode after another in chronological order, as we use it. I witnessed the events in a random sequence, as occurred in Italy, where the only epic and location evidence was the environment, language, and style of clothing, ancient in that case.

In all circumstances my perception, hearing and vision no longer seemed to be physical, they were interspersed between dimensions, as in simply going through a door, or looking through a window. I was able to achieve, in an extraordinary way, a connection beyond human capacity.

Each day that passed, the real events became clearer to me, as they happened in my normal day-to-day life, but without knowing that I was moving between life and death, without reaching the final outcome.

This is how my "journey" inside and outside the hospital took place.

Even though some of the facts reported may seem like mere episodes created by a troubled mind, or fictions reproduced in dreams and nightmares, I was able to perfectly distinguish reality from dreams.

The dreams occurred when my "subconscious" fell asleep, in which I experienced tumultuous situations of escape, persecution, kidnapping, disappointment and death; I would see myself inside of a coffin, or being transported by hearse, unable to move or ask for help, no matter how hard I tried. In nightmares, or simply dreams, the events were disconnected, where one plot joined another completely different one. As supposedly common in such circumstances, there was no beginning or end to the episodes, and they were not so clear.

I don't remember any pleasant dreams that could have comforted me. They were only a reflection of my fears, produced by my tormented subconscious where I saw myself inside of a coffin, or being taken inside of a hearse, or unable to move or speak about being alive.

My turbulent dreams were mostly related to my previous tribulations and were intertwined with my critical state of health.

In the moments when I found myself with active thoughts, or rather, with my mind awake, I listened carefully to what was being said and analyzed everything that was happening around me.

Whether it was a dream or reality, many of these events caused me extreme anguish and I couldn't wait for them to end.

Because I could distinguish one condition from another, between the real and the imaginary, I noticed that after a tumultuous dream my "consciousness awakened" and I sighed with relief, thinking:

- I'm glad it was just a nightmare!

This awakening from the dream was partial, it included only my subconscious, because my body remained unconscious.

I believe that the nightmares did not occur on the same day, however, they were long-lasting and so intense that they seemed to be interconnected. Some of them resembled premonitions, as if they reflected something future. I know this because they occurred later, with the people and situations being the same in their details, but with different scenarios.

Now that the real events in which my presence materialized took place, later, after talking to family and friends involved in my experiences inside and outside the hospital, I learned that both the conversations and the facts happened in the way I had detailed.

Although most of the experiences seem fanciful, or fictitious, similar to science fiction books and films, there is no concrete evidence that I can present that elucidates what happened; except for the episodes that involved other people, whether about the subjects they talked about in my house, where I saw and heard them, as well as during their visits to the hospital, which I reported and which were confirmed.

EYES OPEN

In the early hours of October 7, 2021, my condition changed completely. It was the day I suddenly came out of a coma, in a quick and unique awakening. I opened my eyes and immediately realized that I was alone.

I didn't feel fear, but a sweet relief at being back.

Amidst the night darkness I saw the distant points of external lights, which reflected discreet *flashes* of light around me.

I could see that the room I was in was large, even excessive for just one patient. On the left, attached to a rod, came a device, a wide accordion-shaped hose that went to my mouth and down my throat. I realized that it was a tube for my breathing. A yellowish liquid had accumulated in a bend in the hose and moved, rising and falling according to the respiratory process.

I was afraid that this liquid would return to my lungs.

Without considering the consequences, I wanted to remove the tube, that is, pull it out of my throat, but when I tried to lift my arm to do so, I saw my wrists tied, one on each side of the iron railing of the bed. I insistently pulled my left hand to release the ties. I thought of a plan on how I would do it. I slid my hand several times along the tube to the upper part of the bed's protective bar to try to unhook it through some possible opening, but the attempts were in vain, and besides, I didn't have enough strength to do so. I didn't force my right hand because it had access for IVs and medication. Both hands were very swollen due to the wide and tight bandage around my wrists.

Surely if I could get the restraints off, the first thing I would do was pull the tube out of my throat.

I also began to understand why I often felt like I was in a cave with my hands tied, like a prisoner, everything began to become clearer.

My feet were tingling. I pressed them against the bottom rail of the bed, hoping to stimulate circulation and relieve the uncomfortable lingering cramping sensation.

I didn't feel any pain in any part of my body, but I felt very weak.

I looked to the right, above my head, and saw the equipment that monitored my heartbeat attached to the wall, and next to it, the equipment that monitored my breathing. Below, a container, similar to a bag, hanging from a hook, contained a pasty, light brown liquid, which ran through a thin hose and was inserted into one of my nostrils and into my stomach.

For hours, through the window to my left, I watched the calm of the early morning in the city of Curitiba. It was still dark, but I remembered having seen some of the houses and buildings in the surrounding area on other occasions. For many minutes I watched a flag fluttering in the distance. I recognized that it was from the Paraná Soccer Club stadium.

A thousand thoughts invaded my mind, with a broad evaluation of the facts, from the moment I left home till the recent challenges of my coma, trying to interact with my family members without any feedback.

After centering myself and analyzing parts of what happened, much started to make sense.

Before daylight, a nurse quickly came to the room, but suddenly he fell at the door. With an astonished look he took in my entire situation and remained still for a few seconds.

I don't think he expected to see me awake and even more alive.

As he walked with long strides toward my bed, a suitcase was hanging from his right hand. I noticed that he had come to collect blood. He approached me and, without saying a word, tried to find a prominent vein, but since the area to be punctured between the arm and forearm was purple, he was unsuccessful.

Although I couldn't speak, my gaze and the pain I felt due to the punctures revealed what I was feeling, so he left in a hurry, but without the material.

Some time later the same nurse returned, this time with the best news; that they would intubate me that morning. I couldn't speak because of the tube in my throat, but my face certainly showed an expression of relief.

From that moment on I counted the minutes until I was free from that tube.

I believe that more than an hour had passed and the doctor who was going to come and take the cannula out of my throat had not yet arrived. During this time, I heard the same health professional who had come to collect blood talking to someone in another room:

- Why hasn't the doctor come to remove her tube yet? It's been too long! - *he said indignantly* .

When I heard this comment, I became even more worried, as I was afraid that the liquid from the cannula would return to my lungs and drown me.

A long time had passed until the doctor finally appeared in the room. Three young women accompanied her. I could tell from her posture that she was the young women's teacher and that they had come to watch me being extubated .

They positioned themselves in a semicircle, far from my bed, and watched me for a moment, but the doctor, somewhat embarrassed, called the students to leave the room. It is likely that the fact that I was awake and had my eyes open prevented me from removing the Guedel Cannula at that moment, so I decided to close my eyes and pretend to fall asleep, waiting for them to return.

I stayed like this for a long time, until I heard them return.

The doctor approached my bed and began to instruct the students:

- Look! It's like this - *he pulled the tube, which made a muffled sound, like taking your foot out of mud.*

I had no idea that that moment would be crucial and that I was being exposed to a procedure that, even if necessary, would put me between life and death, or that I could be subjected to a tracheotomy if I did not start breathing again without mechanical assistance.

Although I was outraged by the professional's insensitivity, I felt an immediate sense of relief when the tube was removed. But, to make things worse, after removing the cannula, she immediately put it back in. I don't know why she did that, I started to think that something might have gone wrong.

Everything happened in a fraction of a second and again she removed the tube, which this time slid out of the trachea, coming out easily.

I believe the procedure was to instruct the students to intubate and extubate and, if necessary, perform a tracheotomy.

Fortunately, I was able to breathe again without any blockage.

When I opened my eyes, I could see, despite the mask covering the doctor's mouth and chin, that it was the same doctor who had turned off one of my machines. I even knew her name, which I confirmed by reading her lab coat. My look at her was certainly not the friendliest, because I stared at her with indignation.

Annoyed by my reaction, she looked away and called the young women to leave.

After making sure everything was under control, the students said kind words and left with reverence.

I was left alone, but at least I was untied and without that terrible "pipe" inserted into my throat. It would have been desperate to be awake, and even more so in the previous condition.

I understood that the reason I had my hands tied was necessary, for my protection, so that I wouldn't pull out that cannula, as I had tried to do so.

A feeling of gratitude for being alive and for everything being under control invaded my being... Peace, joy, emotion and warm thoughts emerged and nourished hope in me and calmed my heart.

Because I had always lived Christian principles intensely, during these 21 days of coma I would no longer pray in a conventional way. I maintained a connection with God, as in a conversation between a father and a daughter, by constantly expressing gratitude. This interaction made me feel the fullness of His intercession, which gave me comfort to bear my afflictions.

A nurse came into the room repeatedly to check my glucose and administer medications, which seemed routine to me.

Later a doctor came to talk to me and asked several questions:

- "What is your name?" - *he began* .

I said my first name in a very weak, almost imperceptible voice.

- What's your full name? - *he reinforced*

I replied.

- And your husband's full name?

- Where are you?

I answered all the questions correctly... because they were obvious to me.

– How many children do you have? – *he asked* .

- 21 children... – *I told him, already tired of having talked so much.*

In the state I was in, it seemed to me that the few minutes of this dialogue had been hours of an exhausting interview.

The doctor paused with a suspicious look in my direction and didn't ask any more questions, just wrote something down on his clipboard and said goodbye.

That day, more than one nurse and doctor came to my room, to give me medication or just to observe me. It was as if they came to make sure what had happened and if I had really come out of the coma. That I was alive!

A short, slender, fair-skinned doctor wearing a pink flowered cap approached the ICU and stopped right next to the door. She leaned against the frame and looked at me thoughtfully for a few seconds.

I followed her with an admiring gaze, until finally she spoke:

- Did you know that you are our miracle? You have come back to life! – she *said with a choked voice* – Your blood pressure dropped by 4! – this information was enough to understand part of what had happened to me.

I felt the urge to ask questions, but my voice wouldn't come out, and besides feeling like my throat was sore, I could only emit whispers, almost inaudible.

With a perplexed expression, without saying another word, the doctor left. I was left waiting for the opportunity of when I would see her again.

THE NEW BEGINNING

As the days went by, in recognition of the dedication of each professional, I tried to express my gratitude, even if in whispers, I expressed my gratitude daily, because I knew how much they had worked to help me.

At dusk, a male nurse came to talk to me and together we made a video with a message from me, along with his account of the clinical evolution he had experienced, and forwarded it to my family.

As time went by, in my naive conception, I thought that everything had returned to normal. As if in the "simple" return from the coma I found myself in full physical disposition and vigor, so I wanted to go to the bathroom alone.

I had asked a nurse to accompany me, but she had to rush out to see another doctor. Uncomfortably, because I was wearing a diaper and couldn't stand the abdominal pain, I decided to disconnect some wires that were attached to electrodes on my chest and get out of bed.

As I slid my body to the edge, I fell over the side of the high bed due to weakness. With my body supported on a small ladder, I was left hanging, attached to wires and with no access to my hand. Fortunately, an alarm sounded and they came to help me immediately.

Even though I wasn't hurt or had any major problems, a nurse criticized me with vulgar terms, referring to the stupid thing I had done, but was reprimanded by the nurse who was with her.

Amidst all this confusion , I felt greater empathy for healthcare professionals. The daily challenges they face require a lot of emotional balance to endure them and common sense to know how to proceed in the most adverse situations, as many lives are under their care every day.

The night came quickly, the corridors fell silent.

I didn't like knowing that I would be alone.

I only received the medication that I had received in the early morning, administered by a young nurse who came without a mask. That was the moment I could see that he had features in his physique that reminded me of my son Marcos.

He came over and asked if I wanted the light turned off. I whispered no.

- I understand you! – *he said to me, with a compassionate expression* – I know everything you've been through!...

The boy left in a hurry, but left the light on. After that day I never saw him again.

The fear that someone wanted to harm me, or even kill me, due to the nightmares I had had and the fateful episode with the doctor, still haunted me.

Until late at night I was distracted by listening to a man talking to a child who was hospitalized in the next room. Among other topics and jokes, the two talked about computer games. I remembered seeing an image reflected in the illuminated dome I was in, of a woman with a laptop, who was talking and showing something on the screen to a child.

I spent the whole night practically awake, sometimes looking at the buildings through the window, sometimes at the bathroom mirror about three meters in front of my bed. My thin and haggard face reflected in the mirror described the level to which my illness had reached, however, I still had no idea how long I had spent in hospital.

The first rays of dawn light crept into the room and made me sigh with relief as another day began.

Attached to electrodes that recorded my heart's activity, a blood pressure monitor, an oximeter and a needle with access to my right hand, among other devices I was unfamiliar with, I anxiously awaited getting out of bed.

First a nurse came to take blood, then two cleaning ladies, one of whom was African-American. Despite the mask, I noticed a smile in her eyes and, before leaving, she waved goodbye with a kind gesture. Her gesture showed her contentment at seeing me conscious. I believe she had observed me other times when I was in a coma.

I did not receive food that day, the serum and the preparation that came down through a thin hose, introduced through the nostril, until then, sustained me.

Two nurses silently entered the room and cleaned my bed and me.

It wasn't long before a doctor arrived and transferred his shift to his colleague for the day.

After partially reporting on my clinical progress, the substitute doctor then began to talk to me.

He asked exactly the same questions the other had asked the day before:

- What is your name? ....

I answered them one by one, with confidence ...

- They think I have mental problems, some after-effect, or a blockage in my mind... and they came to test my sanity - *I deduced.*

Due to my privileged memory, which retains vivid memories since I was approximately one and a half years old, if I were asked the date of birth of each child and grandchild and their ages, I would also respond calmly. However, I already imagined that when asked about the number of children, the interrogation would stop.

And that's what happened.

It was to be expected that they would imagine that I was not in full lucidity, because who would have 21 children?

Since my husband had not yet shared details about our family, the medical team did not know that we had 3 biological children and 18 legally adopted children.

The doctor simply said goodbye and left to talk in the hallway with the other doctor. I even imagined what subject they were going to discuss.

During the afternoon they turned on a small, old television, one of those with a picture tube, to distract me, which, despite not having any programs that appealed to me, made the sound and the image alleviate my loneliness.

That same day I heard sobbing and saw a young lady standing in the hallway, near the door to my room. She was crying profusely while a nurse comforted her. From her attitude and desperation, it was clear that a loved one had died.

Before nightfall, I needed to go to the bathroom. A nurse offered to help me get out of bed. As I was getting ready to stand up, with her support, I fell forward with all my weight. The nurse was shorter than me and didn't have enough strength to hold me, which made me fall forward with the IV pole and everything. The fall was strange, as if in "slow motion." I didn't even have a strong impact on the floor. I didn't hurt myself, and neither did the wires or the access to my hand break.

The nurse also fell, but got up quickly and in her desperation went to look for help. It wasn't her fault, because I didn't know that I had lost the feeling in my right leg and foot, which hung downwards, without movement.

As night fell, loneliness came like a whip. The night hours seemed to double, and because I slept so little, my thoughts culminated in fears.

The next day, two nurses helped me out of bed, turned off some machines, put me in a wheelchair and took me to the bathroom. As I went to the bathroom, I could see that my thighs had many circular, purple marks, with small punctures, as if from needles.

At that moment I remembered a nightmare I had had, in which they had fired several shots at my back and legs, which led me to think that the marks could be from this incident and that was why I had been hospitalized.

I asked one of the nurses to take a picture of my back to see if there were any marks there, but to my relief they were clean and very white, so I was sure it was just a dream.

I heard one of them whisper to the other that I must have thought I had wounds on my back, and that it had not been well cared for.

As I still had difficulty maintaining a conversation, I was unable to tell them the reason for my attitude, as I would never question what most of them did for me. I knew how much they dedicated themselves to the care I needed.

I remained alert to obtain information. I wanted to know what had happened to me, even if I didn't know why I ended up in the hospital.

One of the nurses told me that I would be receiving visits from my children, a fact that was no longer news to me. Because of the many experiences I had with them during my coma, I knew exactly which of them would come to see me.

After the bath, I felt as if I had frozen and the discomfort intensified, as if I was about to faint.

I fell asleep for a long time, I was exhausted, getting out of bed had sucked the little energy I had left.

I woke up hours later to a song, sung by the Gilead Quartet:

... " *Hey! Calm down! Everything will be fine!... God is with you... With faith, victory will come*" ...

The lyrics and rhythm of the song penetrated my mind and heart like a balm... I looked to the right and saw my husband, he was wearing a mask, a cap and an orange lab coat. He had turned on the song on his iPhone , at a high volume, and placed it close to my ear.

I felt a mixture of joy and questions, mainly because I knew that he had thought I was going to die, a fact that had passed through the minds of other family members and friends, due to the terrible and discouraging medical information they had received regarding my condition.

My son Juliano was positioned to my left and was holding my hand tightly.

I heard that Juliano had sung to me shortly before, unfortunately I couldn't hear him due to my deep sleep.

What a wonderful sight! To see my son, who lives so far away, in England, there, by my side...and my husband looking at me tenderly.

I remember the first question I asked them:

- Have you paid your employees? Have all the bills been paid?

For someone who was in the process of returning to life, it didn't seem like a timely question at all, nor even the most important one, but it was certainly something that caused me concern.

I felt at ease when they confirmed that everything was okay. Keeping the finances up to date was one of my responsibilities in our company.

Minutes after the two left, the children entered the room: William and then Ozair Neto, the eldest son.

I was overflowing with joy and gratitude to see my male firstborn, by my side; Alive! Before my eyes!

Due to a nightmare I had in which I saw his brutal death and funeral, I absorbed the most intense suffering for a long time, as I imagined I had lost him.

They hugged me... They took pictures with me... I was living a magical moment of indescribable joy.

I really wanted to talk to someone so I could confide in them what had happened to me. Where I had been and what they had told me in other places during the cardiorespiratory arrests and the coma, because I was afraid of forgetting.

The next day, during my daughter Priscila's visit, I had the opportunity to tell her about some special experiences. To my surprise, she recorded part of the conversation on video. Unfortunately, I couldn't talk much, as I was very weak.

I also received a visit from my son Bruno. It was on that day that I started eating a kind of creamy soup, but after the first few spoonfuls I choked and coughed compulsively... I remembered that the day before, when I was coughing and releasing a lot of secretions, I heard loud laughter coming from another room and a nurse made fun of me and said that my cough sounded like his dog's. I felt embarrassed, but I didn't value the unfortunate comment.

Bruno helped me eat the chicken soup, because I didn't have the strength in my hands to lift the spoon. I was overjoyed to hear him say, with tears in his eyes, that I had taken care of him and that now it was his turn.

I was blessed with yet another day of great emotion and special attention, which provided me with a greater amount of physical and emotional healing.

UNCONDITIONAL LOVE

As I regained my strength, my husband told me part of what happened during the coma.

He told me that visitors were not allowed at the hospital due to Covid . He also told me that shortly before they extubated me for the first time, they explained to him the risks of this procedure, in order to make him aware, and that this extubation was not successful and I had another cardiorespiratory arrest .

After much insistence, two days before coming out of the coma, he managed to get some of my children, those who lived further away, to be allowed to see me.

My husband, William and Marcelo were initially allowed.

Marcelo felt sick when he saw me in that deplorable condition and couldn't stand to stay in the room. He staggered until he managed to sit down on a chair in the hallway. William just watched me from a distance, as instructed by his father.

This visit represented a final farewell for them and it happened in the same way as I had seen it, different because of the location, because while I was observing them, as in the previous report, I felt like I was in a tunnel under the sidewalk between the vegetable garden and the living room of my house.

Soon after coming out of the coma, my husband had the opportunity to tell the medical team that we had 21 children.

Most of them lived in England and Europe and would soon need to return to their families and work.

It was on this occasion that the doctors learned that I had told the truth about the number of children I had and that I had not been affected by some degeneration of the brain cells as they had imagined.

The daily bulletins given to family members by telephone were always demotivating:

That I would not survive due to the new complications that my condition presented every day and, if by some miracle I survived, I would be left with irreversible neuromotor sequelae , which is common in similar cases.

My daughter Eloise , who lives in the United States and cannot be with me, received, precisely on her birthday, the sad news that the doctors could do nothing more for me, that all we could do was wait.

Even though my children were aware that they could lose their jobs and would have to leave their families for an indefinite period of time, they still made every effort to make the long trip to be with me and their father, regardless of the losses. My daughter, who lived in Campinas (São Paulo), with her husband and four children, managed to come the day after I was admitted. Eloise , who lives in the US, really wanted to be with me, but due to issues at the university where she was studying for her Master's degree, she was unable to do so, and the same thing happened to my son Rodrigo, who lives in northern Italy.

The altruistic attitude and affection, even if some of them expressed it from a distance, contributed significantly to my recovery.

The energy that came from the prayers, fasting, consideration and love that they gave me, despite not being able to visit me, not only provided well-being, but also the power to heal. Not to mention that their presence strengthened my husband who was desolate. They were able to go out with him and keep him company during this difficult time.

As my health gradually recovered, four days later, on October 11, 2021, I was transferred from the Intensive Care Unit to a ward. They removed the tube from my nostril and I began to eat more soft foods and drink water. They kept only the electrodes, blood pressure monitor, and access to IV fluids and medications.

The physiotherapy and breathing exercises that I have been doing since the third day after I came out of the coma have helped me to strengthen my legs and my breathing.

I remained alone in the ward until nightfall, when two patients were brought into the room. Later I received a visit from my sister who had come to be my companion.

The next day a doctor came to evaluate me, and her empathy and kindness caught my attention. I didn't hesitate to ask her to discharge me, explaining that I wanted to enjoy the company of my children before they left. She said that she would only let me go home when she no longer saw me lying in bed.

After the doctor left, I realized that she was the same doctor who had seen me at the door of the Intensive Care Unit and said that I was alive by a miracle. She had overseen the entire resuscitation process when I was admitted to the hospital.

On the first night in the ward, I couldn't sleep because of the continuous and annoying conversations of the companions of the other two patients. Since I had no other alternative, I spent hours planning what I would do the next day.

Setting goals, writing books, journaling, reading, listening to uplifting speeches, making plans and studying languages have always been part of my favorite habits. When I don't feel well, whether physically or emotionally, or simply because I'm losing sleep, these pleasant subterfuges help me clear my head and push away bad thoughts.

This is what happened during that long night. Although the plans were not written in a notebook or typed, they helped to distract me.

The day dawned, my sister , as always, helpful and attentive, and another woman, who was accompanying another patient, helped me to go to the bathroom and then made me sit on the sofa, as I had asked them to. I wanted the doctor to see me "out of bed", as she had told me, so that she could release me.

I drew strength from where it seemed to have none and remained seated with determination.

I was aware that I was not in a position to receive care at home, but my desire to spend time with my children would outweigh the risks, at least that was what I thought at the time.

The tiredness tripled due to being poorly accommodated, but being released, whatever the cost, to be with the family was still a priority.

My husband arrived early, in the meantime my sister left.

I was so anxious that I kept asking someone what time it was. Three hours had already passed and the doctor still hadn't come. I found out that she would only be able to evaluate me at lunchtime. Despite my expectations, I had to go back to bed because I couldn't stand the fatigue.

When the doctor arrived, my husband told her that I had refused, for a long time, to get off the couch so that she could see me there and discharge me so that I could be with the children. - they both laughed - And to my joy, she then released me.

It was just time to sort out the hospital discharge paperwork, change my clothes and head to my precious home.

Settled into a wheelchair, as I headed to the car, I took a close look at the things around me. I was familiar with each environment: the hallway, the elevator, until I ended up on the outdoor patio. Vague memories emerged of when I arrived semi-conscious at the hospital, being put in a wheelchair, and some time later my husband helping me to go to the bathroom. After that, only when I found myself "imprisoned" in a small space under a slab.

So, little by little, flashes of memories of other places I had been to came back to me.

Anxious to get home and hug my children , I tried not to dwell on these memories, I focused only on what was most important at the moment.

The sweet feeling of rebirth accompanied me throughout the journey, until my husband placed me in the front seat of the car.

On the way home, with the seat reclined, I contemplated, in wonder, the grandeur of the blue sky, the trees in their earthly power, the real beauty of the flowers... everything seemed more vibrant, more intense, as if I were visualizing the things around me with a different interpretation, absorbing all their magnitude.

My hearing remained sharp, my eyes even purer and my thoughts smoother and more organized.

This new perception was mixed with the magnitude of the feeling of gratitude.

I was overjoyed, filled with emotion and love for God, for His infinite goodness, which had manifested itself in the miracles and experiences of sublime and significant value that I had lived and which should never be forgotten or doubted.

As soon as we got home, my son Juliano, as always attentive, ran to the car to help my husband carry me to the living room. Since I had lost 20 kg, my 50 kg did not require much effort.

I sighed with emotion when I saw most of my family and the beautiful reception they prepared for me. At the top of the large window of the winter garden, large heart-shaped balloons with the phrase, in English and Portuguese: " *Welcome Mom ! We love you* ", demonstrating the joy they felt at my return.

My daughter Luciana and her children, William, Juliano, Ozair Neto, Marcelo, my friend Rosangela and my husband, were waiting for me, beaming and visibly excited. Priscila and her two children, Bruno and his son had to travel the day before.

As they sat me down in the most comfortable chair in the dining room, they placed a crown, with replicas of rubies embedded around it, on my head, which made me feel like a true queen. For a while, sitting in a semicircle, they watched me silently. Their faces showed that they still could not believe that they were seeing me... Alive! Sitting in front of them!

The silence was interrupted by William, the most lively son of the family, and my husband who started joking around to relax, took photos and filmed...

The weakness and extreme discomfort did not prevent me from giving discreet smiles and mumbling a few words.

It is impossible to describe exactly the emotion and joy that continued to invade my soul. There are no words or actions that can express the reality of what happened to me during those 27 days filled with unbelievable events.

Immersed in the most sublime gratitude, at no time did I lament, murmur, or question the reason for everything that had happened to me, but on the contrary, I felt as if I were picking spring roses in the depths of winter. I valued only the miracle itself, provided by the power of God that had acted upon me throughout this period, by healing me and restoring my life.

Despite being awake the whole time, I spent that night overjoyed to be home. I only blinked because of the uncomfortable pain in my right leg and foot and my difficulty breathing. My children and husband also couldn't sleep. They were anxious and worried about me. They came into my room all the time to help me take my blood pressure, measure my glucose, temperature and oxygen levels, and talk to me to help me relax.

At dawn, a tightness came into my heart...

Saying goodbye to my lovely boys was painful. With sad eyes but grateful hearts, the four of them hugged me, said loving words and headed to the airport.

I recognized that their presence and affection were the additional strength for my recovery, even more so because I knew all the time, even in a coma, that the children who maintained a greater connection with me were the same ones I could see nearby. This was one of the factors that motivated me to continue in the battle for life.

My eldest daughter, Luciana, stayed with her four boys to help me with the care I needed. We spent a few days on the coast of Paraná with her family.

Her undivided attention and the affection of her grandchildren, combined with the healthy and nutritious food she prepared, accelerated my recovery.

Despite the intense pain and numbness in my lower limbs, I was able to move around. I hopped around, using my left leg more, and leaned against the walls and furniture in the house. My husband insisted on getting me a wheelchair to make me more comfortable, but I didn't agree; not only because I had seen myself confined to a wheelchair too many times, but also because I knew I would need to encourage mobility.

Everything was going well, until; on the fourth day at home, during the early hours of the morning, I was struck by intense chest pain, a pain like I had never felt before.

My husband made me sit on the sofa in the living room, and then we went to the hospital. My daughter was already by my side and her look described her fears.

The pain intensified, I let out a loud groan and felt like I was about to have a heart attack.

Absorbed by such anguish, I imagined that nothing more could be done. That I had survived only so that I could say goodbye to my family and receive a little attention and affection. As I anticipated, once again, my final moments, I cried out once more for my life. My husband also prayed and pronounced a blessing of healing and comfort.

I was in this condition for a few minutes, until the pain stopped, instantly, as if nothing had happened.

At dawn we returned to Colombo, where we live, in order to be close to the cardiology hospital where we have our insurance. On the other hand, because we live on a farm surrounded by the Atlantic forest, with dense humidity, the pain in my leg and foot worsened.

At that time Luciana returned to her house.

Her support was essential for my recovery. Her attention and concern for my health helped me regain much of my strength and gain weight.

Day after day, I would overcome the difficulty in walking and breathing. The bedsores on my head caused gaps that I was able to hide with my own hair, while the weakness that persisted due to severe anemia was cured months later with appropriate foods and supplements. I did not need a transfusion as requested by a doctor.

Since many memories of experiences I had during cardiorespiratory arrest and in the coma began to come back to me, even with many limitations and with great difficulty, I began to write them down in my diary, as I was still worried that I would forget them.

Of everything I had experienced, no matter how many reasons there were, I still had nothing to complain about.

By seeing adversity as a source of learning and personal evolution, tribulations became lighter, and I acquired greater emotional capacity to deal with new challenges and extra motivation to move forward without looking back.

WHAT DO YOU WANT ME TO DO?

These events, according to a clinical opinion, would certainly be defined as outbreaks caused by neurons, due to the great trauma that I had suffered, or as pareidolia , which is a psychological phenomenon, in which a reaction that occurs in the brain produces random stimuli that combine imagination with science, and makes people see faces or inanimate objects. This opinion does not match my case, due to what I experienced and its evidence; except for when my subconscious reproduced the image of a cave for the ICU and when I felt inside of a bubble, which represented the medical devices connected to my body.

However, as much as these experiences may attract the most varied points of view, be they the most skeptical, scientific, disbelieving, or introspective, and even fail to meet the reader's expectations, the existence of a Creator, a caring Father, was evident in each situation. Whether between cardiac arrests, during the coma, or during convalescence, the miracle was confirmed.

Under no circumstances do I dare say that everything happened this way by simple coincidence, by chance, or by luck, as such occurrences are commonly assessed. It was clear that these were measures taken by God and his "entourage", his angels, or messengers, as they are better called. They also inspired the medical team to persevere and take the correct procedures.

When reflecting on the reasons for having lived through so many adverse situations, which caused me despair, fear and the terrible feeling of confinement, one can imagine that the transition from life to death can be something fearful, or that it always follows this pattern. I also don't think that I was being subjected to some condemnatory sentence, because throughout my life I maintained standards between what is fair, correct and dignified.

Certainly everything that happened had a wise purpose, not only of learning, but as if I were participating in a test, where I needed to extract all the strength from within me to exercise self-control, confidence, perseverance, patience, courage, faith and even greater gratitude.

What had the greatest impact on things happening this way was that during the cardiac arrests and the initial period of the coma I did not understand what was happening. For this reason my subconscious created scenarios to represent the premise of my fears; where the ICU room sometimes seemed like a cave or a tunnel, environments that had always been hostile to me. The bed itself and the equipment around me took the imaginary form of a "transparent bag", where I felt like I was a large fetus.

Although the justifications within science contribute to explaining much of what occurred, it is very clear that there was a very distinct set of procedures and factors, which, associated with the Master's final touch, changed the course of what had previously been defined as irreversible.

These circumstances, which are not so common, confirm that the reversal of a critical clinical condition, or even death, does not occur by itself. After all the technical means and involvement of professionals, such a process is completed through a greater power, where the intervention is no longer human, but rather, of God.

Because some friends and loved ones interacted in their prayers with this Glorious Being and expressed their desire for my recovery, through their belief and devotion, regardless of each person's religion, whether through prayers or fasting, combined with my intense desire to live, they were answered and contributed to the miracle being realized, however, in accordance with God's will.

When I refer to the word miracle, I emphasize its meaning not only as an event that occurred outside the ordinary, inexplicable by the laws of nature, but that it is very clear and obvious to those who believe in something intangible. Only those who have already lived through similar situations can understand the magnitude of such experiences.

Among the moments that involved faith and perseverance, I remember hearing my son Juliano think, however, the sensation was as if he were whispering in my ear:

- Remember when mom said that prayer and fasting have power!
- *I was moved to hear these truths spoken, or thought by my son.*

Even though the first nights at home were plagued by pain, weakness and difficulty breathing, associated with constant feelings of fainting, such difficulties did not prevent me from staying in tune with God, seeking answers and guidance.

One of these troubled mornings, I got up as usual. Quietly so as not to disturb my husband, I leaned against the bed and then against the wall, and so on until I reached the living room. Despite taking painkillers, the throbbing pain in my right leg and foot did not stop. I settled down on the retractable sofa to raise my legs and placed cushions under my feet to improve blood circulation.

After I was in relative comfort, I turned my thoughts fervently to prayer. My requests were not only that the pain would stop, but that I would also be guided in what else I needed to do in my extended days.

I kept up this loving and thoughtful conversation for many minutes.

Immersed in emotion, I remained in supplication as I had done other times, and I waited for the moment when the answers would come. Sometimes I prayed out loud and other times, in my thoughts.

- What do you want me to do? – *I asked, waiting for guidance.*

Because I had been deserving of such mercy and kindness, and had been given another chance to live on Earth, I wanted to give back and wanted to know how I could do so.

I remained focused on my request for a long time. I knew that Heavenly Father was there, present, as He had been many times in the hospital, comforting and protecting me.

I was ready and willing to do anything that might be required of me.

As I expected; it didn't take long for an answer to flash and overwhelm my senses.

A song of praise was sung to me.... It flowed into my thoughts with the sweetest sensation arising from the genuine love of an omnipresent Father. Absorbed by that angelic choir, I felt the words and music sound harmonious and penetrate my entire being.

The chorus clearly showed the orientation, or a purpose:

Father, grant us light,

It does us good to live;

Illuminate our gaze, make us understand,

We want the mission to spread the light.

Give us such a mission Lord,

Give us, O Jesus!

My attention was drawn to the meaning of each verse which elicited an instant response:

– I need to live well and spread the Light! – Yes, I do! How? – *I thought* .

Overcome by the deepest emotion, tears rolled down my face and smiles of relief flooded my soul.

The answer came subtly, yet readily, like something simple and obvious:

The example, words, actions and spreading the teachings of Jesus Christ with greater emphasis would be a way to live well, to be a "Light" and to spread it. I have always been committed to this cause. Spreading the gospel was a constant motto in my life, however, upon understanding the direction exposed on that occasion, my understanding expanded when such temporal and eternal designs were pointed out.

This was not the first time I had received some guidance through a chant.

In mid-September 2018, when we were living in São Lourenço do Sul, in Rio Grande do Sul, and doing voluntary service as missionaries, I had health problems and had difficulty breathing, associated with dizziness and extreme fatigue.

At the time we were going through family disappointments, which caused me annoyance and a lot of stress, when, through a song, right in the first verse, I was alerted to the seriousness of my illness:

"Prolong the good times,

That are draining away,

Enjoy the radiant sun,

The night will come!"

Our efforts cannot stop the afterglow...

The answer came as lightning and cleared my mind.

- Why not more precise guidance?

My moments were running out... It was a warning that we would have to take urgent action.

That day we didn't hesitate, we went straight to the Emergency Room at the hospital in the small town. After a worrying diagnosis involving heart problems, in a race against time, we traveled for 3 hours to a hospital in Porto Alegre. Where I underwent more detailed tests and received a report of a heart attack and pulmonary embolism. I was sent to the Intensive Care Unit and received the appropriate treatment.

I remember that, on his first visit, the doctor, with an admiring expression, said:

- You are a very lucky woman!

Due to having received "a heavenly message" through a song, combined with faith and not delaying in seeking resources, the doctor's statement would better suit the adjective: "you are a *very blessed woman* ."

~~~~

The pain ceased completely. I felt peace flow like a calm dawn breeze; that true peace described in the Master's words:

" *My peace I leave with you, and not as the world gives do I give unto you...*"

And as in other moments when Jesus greeted:

"Peace be with you!"

Our Savior's desire is to provide us with peace, we just need to be in tune with Him to understand how to obtain it.

I was able to fully understand what the gift of promised peace would be like, which is extended to those who believe.

Because it is a heavenly gift, peace goes far beyond the feeling of tranquility that we know.

I fell asleep right there, on the couch, amazed by everything I was experiencing.

EVERYTHING FITS

The next day I did not hesitate to report these special experiences and others to my husband. His posture and astonished look showed that he did not disbelieve any of my stories.

All the things I witnessed in the hospital and outside were confirmed by him and, later, by my children:

My husband's conversation with the couple of friends about pizza. When he mentioned getting dressed after my death happened as I had seen and told him. My son Juliano singing outside the house with his friend, next to the car.

The only difference between the facts was that they were in our house and not in the hospital as I imagined.

I also heard about William and Marcelo's visit to my hospital room. It was the day I felt sad because they didn't stay or talk to me, when I felt like I was in a tunnel.

My daughter Priscila's birthday celebration, when I asked why I wasn't celebrating with them. It happened as I had witnessed, the difference was that I was watching them from below, as I felt like I was in a cave below the sidewalk.

My husband confirmed that on the first night I was in a coma, he sat in the armchair in the living room and, desolate, thought about everything that had happened to me, while I was sitting on the other side, on the larger sofa, and witnessed his grief.

The memory of much of what had happened remained vivid, however, when in a coma, I did not understand why my family and other people did not see me or talk to me, much less why my children had come from another country and were staying at my house.

When I saw my renovated house, without the winter garden, it was the period in which I reached a greater understanding of what was happening, I knew that I could not make myself present, or make anyone see me.

As incredible as it may seem, this restructuring of the house took place two years later, and it was intended for commercial use.

When I saw my son Marcos and his wife, despite being in their own home, I felt as if they were right next to me and I heard them talking about their everyday family matters.

My understanding during the first cardiac arrest in which I ended up under a narrow floor was that "my spirit came out from under the stretcher" and I was in a space where I could only crawl, from where I saw the doctor and the silhouettes of other people who were performing resuscitation on me. I felt materialized in that narrow space, and I was unaware of my ability to leave there and go anywhere else, because I had no idea that I had died.

Because I couldn't see my body, I spent a long time without knowing what was happening.

In almost every circumstance I felt debilitated and trapped in a dark place, unable to participate or interact with anyone. The tunnel I imagined myself in, underground, in the vision of a comatose patient, could be a pertinent description for an ICU.

Despite the attention and care I received, my mind portrayed that room as a melancholic place, due to the loneliness, the suffering and the fact that I was unable to leave there.

As for the man who turned on one of the machines that kept me alive, I didn't know who he was, nor did I see him leave the room, but I remained certain that it was divine providence.

Since visits were not allowed in the Intensive Care Unit, due to my clinical condition and the Coronavirus infestation , my husband insisted on more than one occasion to see me, and they allowed it once, only after I said that he was not there as my husband, but rather as a religious leader, my "pastor", which he really was.

Only with this argument, which was in line with the hospital management's visiting protocol, did they authorize him to see me.

As soon as he entered the room, he was faced with my appalling condition.

As he observed me, he touched my cold, swollen body and noticed that I did not react to any stimulus and did not even show a movement or tremor... From then on, he understood why the doctors' reports were discouraging.

His visits occurred when I felt immersed in a bag of water and saw him looking at me. He remained by my side for a few minutes and then left in the company of a young man, who was a nurse.

Even though the environments seemed enigmatic, I witnessed all these episodes in some way, when looking at people, even if they were very far away, or when "my other self", or my spirit, moved around the hospital room and other places.

Everything that happened resembled normal life, with the only difference being that I could neither be seen nor heard, because in no moment I emitted the sound of my voice, I would only interact with the thoughts and conversations of others. I lived like this for 21 days.

In between the 5 cardiorespiratory arrests reported by the doctors, which occurred on alternate days, was when the near-death experiences would occur. During one of them, probably the longest NDE, lasting more than 16 minutes, I was allowed to exercise my free will, in which I was able to decide to return to life.

Months later, I had access to reports of near-death experiences, after telling part of what had happened to a friend and she suggested that I research the subject on the internet. From there I obtained information about NDEs .

All these events were mixed together in periods that we call past, present and future, or yesterday, today and tomorrow; However, in my new understanding, during the coma, I no longer differentiated the passing of time as we understand it. Everything occurred as something unique, without divisions of seconds, minutes, hours, days, months. There was also no chronological sense; so much so that, when I woke up 21 days later, despite having retained several memories, it seemed to me that there was no gap between times.

When making a comparison based on the "speed" factor of everything that was happening to me, this experience could be explained, in some aspects, by Einstein's theory of relativity of time, which states: that when a body begins to move and gain speed in the dimension of space, the speed of time decreases for it, passing more slowly, that is, the faster a body moves, the slower time passes, and it becomes relative. In a certain way that is how it was, time seemed to extend as my rapid transportations occurred.

From the information reported by my husband, I learned that during the initial treatment at the Emergency Room, they arranged several tests, including heart tests, blood tests and others. After obtaining the results, they said they found nothing abnormal in me.

During this time of waiting and observation, more than 2 hours passed. They asked him many questions, in fact an interrogation about my psychological condition, because they thought I was just emotionally shaken.

Ozair explained that everything was fine at the moment regarding the children and marital relationship and that we had a trip scheduled for the following week. He also told me about the recent procedures I had undergone on my heart. That I was a LADA diabetic, that I had had COVID but was asymptomatic and that I had chosen not to be immunized. He talked about the procedures and comorbidities, hoping that such information could contribute to a more accurate diagnosis.

While the doctor, who seemed somewhat inexperienced, insisted on the psychological issue, my condition worsened. At this time, someone informed another doctor, who was on the 5th floor, about my condition. He quickly came down, put me on a stretcher and rushed me to the Intensive Care Unit.

My husband, without realizing what was happening, managed to see the doctor pass by him quickly and followed him, but they didn't let him enter the room, he could only wait in the hallway.

As my vital signs had disappeared, or rather, my heart and breathing had stopped, they began resuscitation procedures and intubated me.

The next day they diagnosed me with diabetic ketoacidosis and candidiasis that had lodged itself in my urinary system. This acidity, or ketones in my blood, traveled throughout my body and damaged my organs, even causing cardiorespiratory arrest.

In addition to the cardiac arrests, at one point during the coma my kidneys stopped working, on two other occasions my lungs filled with water.

Due to these complicated situations that were beyond their control, the doctors remained convinced that my chances of survival were zero or minimal. As I previously reported, if a miracle were to occur, I would be left with irreparable after-effects. In this way, the daily bulletins transmitted to family members continued.

Despite the suffering, I feel grateful, because everything contributed to making it possible for me to share many of my experiences, from the incomparable mercy and love of Our Heavenly Father, to the persistence of the medical team, for not giving up, even with the most prolonged cardiorespiratory arrests, in which they continued with resuscitation maneuvers.

When I pondered the events in the spiritual sphere, I understood that there were more reasons for me not to continue on the sublime and inviting path that showed me a new and more abundant life, which I am not fully aware of, but which I will certainly discover in the course of my life.

In the circumstances in which I found myself between cardiorespiratory arrests; the power of God was manifested, through miracles, which were carried out, not only to strengthen those who believe and to testify to non-believers, but also for my own improvement.

From all the experiences I have had, whether the most distressing or the ones that brought me a sense of well-being, I have learned and I have an even greater desire to continue firmly in my purpose of staying close to God and the teachings of Jesus Christ, that is: "Stay close to the tree", as I was instructed to do while I was in cardiac arrest, as well as benefit other people in some way, and confirm the existence of God and his immense love for us.

A NEW PERSPECTIVE

Something wonderful happened in the four months after I was discharged, during which time I felt as if I were walking on clouds. This incredible sensation of floating, I describe not as something physical, but as an advanced understanding, as if I were no longer on earth and its tribulations.

I felt free from futile and meaningless things, where nature seemed to have absorbed an extraordinary beauty, a different splendor, that I had not noticed before. Gratitude had become personified as an inexhaustible source of love and hope.

No fear would come over me whatsoever, much less of death; my inner peace and security seemed endless. Information concerning human life and the world to come flowed serenely through my thoughts.

I literally noticed myself as being reborn, as if I had become a new person. Not that I was a bad person, but I had become stronger, not in terms of physical strength, but in terms of emotional and spiritual strength, where my thoughts became more elevated and altruistic.

Because I had been, throughout my life, a woman who was overly sensitive to rude attitudes and worried about negative criticism, with the new heavenly teachings I had received, I began to feel covered by God's protection and more fearless in the face of setbacks.

This simplified way of thinking and acting made me see the deficiencies in human attitudes in a different way; where mistakes, vulgarities, harsh words, petty thoughts, evil, or any insane attitudes remained in his quadrant of the unacceptable.

When I was in a coma, in total vulnerability, I felt the desire to scream for help, so that they wouldn't turn off the equipment, or so that they would come to my aid. In the current situation I feel the desire to "scream", as a cry of warning so that many change the condemnable course of their lives and give value to what matters most, before it is too late.

Even though, in my opinion, the answers or solutions to any difficulty were clear, I regretted that many, including family members, did not realize the best and happiest way to live. Where rocky paths, with obscure access, could be replaced with well-defined trails, accompanied by "guides", "compasses" and whole firm orientation.

The mistakes we make along our path, because we think we have something material, that we own something, or are superior to someone, leads us to forget that everything was lent to us for a period of time. That we are all equal; equal in the sense of existence, that is, with the same beginning and end in this life.

The wrongful use of free agency produces blindness which affects a big part of humanity and causes all kinds of unpleasantness and even irreparable loss. The sacrifice and teachings of our Master act to entice reflection, the abandonment of insane practices and to lead us to a restart through repentance and forgiveness.

As I immersed myself in so many reflections, a wealth of meaningful thoughts took shape and began to define what I should strive for. My goals were refined and material aspirations took on their ephemeral value.

I spent this entire period in meditation. Many things became clear as I pondered or read with this perspective and a vast array of understanding opened up, which is not limited to the period of this life, but also to the world to come.

These and other inspirations that I have mentioned flooded my mind daily like a beam of light, to the point where I no longer felt like I was standing on solid ground. I didn't even realize the complexity of life; everything seemed obvious, logical, easier or without complications. I felt as if "windows to another dimension", to a better world, were half-open.

Even if I were to use all the words possible to describe what was happening, I would not be able to even begin to imitate the reality I was experiencing, as they were not random thoughts, much less common experiences, but rather, something that cannot be understood with a simple personal analysis, or with a logic view.

Despite having retained much understanding and having my faith reinvigorated with this "life lesson", unfortunately, as I feared, over time much of the immensity of knowledge from beyond this life was gradually overshadowed by the change in focus, due to everyday circumstances having been resumed.

My greatest wish would be to have remained in that elevated state of spirit and understanding, and to have continued my life in perfect harmony with everything and everyone around me.

During this period I felt lighter, no negative or critical thoughts crossed my mind. This complete liberation from the world produced true happiness in my days of convalescence. If I had to define it in a simplified way, I would say that they were "magical moments".

It was a period in which all my senses and my life turned exclusively to God and illuminated my thoughts, providing greater peace and understanding. I felt protected from external negative influences, as if I had achieved perfect balance between mind and body.

Surprisingly, this intervention spread among the people I know, leading them to reflect more carefully on their attitudes and way of living, at least at this stage in which they witnessed unprecedented events.

FREEDOM OF CHOICE

" *You Decide* "; a phrase with a simple connotation, but with a relevant meaning, because it refers to the possibility of a choice.

As I walked towards a new life plan, I was given the chance to choose, and to this day the answer I heard: "You Decide", said at the moment I was in one of the cardiac arrests, echoes in my thoughts and remains in my considerations, as it resonates in a more detailed analysis of each decision to be made.

As our decisions shape our lives, in my moment of near death, even though it was a decision that was not completely in my hands, I was presented with the possibility of choosing to live for a longer period of time.

An opportunity, which was granted to me, that was filled with learning and opened my mind to better understand why adversity occurs and what we need to achieve a greater level of balance between mind and body.

Our lives, as well as those of the people around us, are directly and indirectly impacted by our decisions. Freedom of choice is a gift, and its consequences can be long-lasting, both for our happiness and for our general decline. Therefore, nothing good or bad happens in our lives without having been previously influenced by our choices.

Because our destiny is tied to the decisions we make throughout our lives, I think it is of fundamental importance to focus more on the outcome of what we desire, in order to be more cautious in the use of our free will.

The mistaken application of free will produces results that can bring, in addition to much sadness, even irreparable losses.

As an antidote to heal the wounds caused by bad choices, the sacrifice and teachings of Our Master can lead us to reflect and abandon senseless practices and lead us to a new beginning through repentance and forgiveness.

The remarkable and valuable experience that I have lived has provided a new perspective on life, as well as the opportunity to share such events and precepts, with the purpose of contributing, in a concise and inspiring way, a warning for our next attitudes, in which I include myself in.

THE ROUTINE THAT FOLLOWS

Still weak, in November, I arranged for a cardiology and blood tests and consulted with specialists to find out if I would be able to travel, as I had not given up on my plans. I really wanted to be with most of my children for my birthday, Christmas and the New Year.

Despite our concerns, we bought the ticket and traveled at the end of the month.

As expected, I arrived in Manchester, UK , literally dragging myself along. Pain and weakness had taken over my body. I felt very sick during the flight, but I tried to keep my mind focused on my purpose so as not to despair.

To make up for it, we had some incredible days. We stayed at the home of my son Juliano and his wife Gabriela for a month. My birthday was wonderful, it felt like I was celebrating my first year of life.

The apartment was packed, not only with family, but with the love that radiated in smiles and lively conversations.

The Christmas and New Year festivities added more happiness to our family stay, which concluded with a visit to our son Rodrigo and his wife and son in Italy.

Even with my unfavorable health condition, associated with uncomfortable pain in my left shoulder, which had started during the trip and made it difficult to move my arm, I was still able to happily enjoy these special moments.

I later learned that this injury was caused by having forced my arm in an attempt to untie my left hand which was tied to the bed rail, after having come out of a coma in the ICU.

Fortunately, this illness was soon resolved.

A SHARP PERCEPTION

Due to the fact that I remained unconscious for so many days, under the effect of strong medications, even if I was not subjected to morphine, or anything similar, many may imagine that the facts reported result from hallucinations, or daydreams due to the deep coma, or paranoia due to the illnesses, or simply insanity. Whatever the assumption, there is no concrete evidence to prove the events and places that I saw and was, except for the confirmation of the people involved in my visions.

Only a person who has gone through a similar experience can interpret or feel the magnitude of the knowledge that is obtained under such conditions.

Unconcerned with any opposing opinion, I focused on the new understanding and learning I had obtained, maintaining the firm conviction that we are not alone in this vast universe and that our journey on Earth does not mean just birth, growth, create a family that will have an end when we die and that's it, everything is over.

But yes, life continues after we leave our body.

The 5 cardiorespiratory arrests due to serious illnesses and consecutive resuscitations, 3 of them on different days, in addition to the prolonged coma and having survived, as well as the information in the medical records, are evidence of the miracle that occurred.

There was a first attempt at extubation , which was unsuccessful, and I suffered another cardiorespiratory arrest.

Since the bulletins updated every day did not give my family any hope, they were left to wait for the worst.

During the first cardiac arrest I was below the hospital floor and probably for the longest time, that's when I found myself in the "illuminated portal."

As I drowned, huddled in what I imagined to be "a large placenta", which was filling with water, that was when the sirens went off because my lungs were filling with water... And then the tapotagens occurred , or the "slaps" I received on the back, to help clear the obstruction in my lungs.

My heart had withstood many attacks by the fact that in June of the same year, three months before the coma, I had undergone a catheterization and angioplasty, due to the arteries being almost completely obstructed. But my heart also withstood all of it by divine grace.

In an emergency procedure, due to chest pain, they placed 6 stents , in addition to the other 3 stents from a previous angioplasty. This procedure helped my heart withstand subsequent cardiac arrests and other illnesses.

After a year and a half of reflection, I decided to extract from my diary and my memories the facts as they occurred, in their entirety, and write them down to make this extremely important part of my life public. I did this with the purpose of contributing in some way, either with the absolute certainty obtained about our existence after this life, or that we have a Creator who wishes to interact with us, if we allow it.

As a writer, this would be my fourth literary work, but since I was still debilitated due to weakness and constant chest pain, I decided to quickly and succinctly write a book intended only for family and a few friends who had witnessed the event, as I was afraid that I would have a heart attack and would not have enough time to finish the work due to progressive atherosclerosis. While I was writing, I underwent another catheterization and angioplasty due to a blocked stent , but I still finished this book "You Decide", with a few copies that I distributed to a select audience.

I gave one of these copies to the cardiologist who has been following my clinical condition for 4 years. Later, during one of his appointments, he told me that he and his wife had read my book. In his comment, he mentioned the courage I had had to write such accounts. When I saw his admiring but not skeptical expression, I realized that by referring to it as an act of courage to have written such controversial facts, which do not fit with human logic or science, they could be interpreted as dreams or figments of the imagination, since there is no more concrete evidence, and therefore they would not be credible.

After recovering, I resumed writing and managed to write it in a more elaborate manner and with new spelling corrections.

During this time of reflection and production of my work, I learned about other people, close to the family, who had similar experiences to mine, however, each with their own peculiarities.

From everything I experienced, some warnings were instilled in my mind, among them:

*It is not always the case that when your family member or friend is in a coma, hopeless, with an apparently irreversible condition, that he is about to die, or dead. He or she may be in despair, trying to let you know that he or she is alive, begging you to continue with the care, procedures, as well as with the machines connected.

*That the love and attention of the family radiate upon the sick person, providing the balm of healing.

It is worth noting that, since the beginning of 2020, until the period in which I was convalescing, thousands of lives had been lost due to the Coronavirus and its implications, however, many of them due to a lack of resources, or because the resource that kept them alive had been taken away, in order to sustain another life that had greater prospects of survival.

In my early mornings of pain and pondering, I remembered some biblical verses, among them, in Proverbs 31 that refers to the value of a virtuous woman, which can be extended to men, who, by paying due attention to God's commandments, can surpass rubies.

In Isaiah 54:12, when referring to the church of Jesus Christ, which even though was devastated, would be exalted: "... *I will make your windows clear, your gates of rubies, and all your borders of fine stones.*"

Such analogies give us a glimpse of what may be within our reach, according to our merits.

It is rewarding to follow paths of personal righteousness, as we follow the Light that is Christ, Jesus. As much as other paths may seem more attractive and fun, they are nothing more than mirages in a scorching desert.

From the alert I had on the "portal":

- *If you continue you will never come back!*

Although it represents a passage to the other world or another existence, this "portal" can serve as a reflection on the paths and decisions we make throughout our lives, which if they are dark, with a contradictory effect to what drives our physical and spiritual well-being, the answer may be:

- *" We won't be back."*

And the option:

- *You decide!*

If we remain in our comfort zone, or persist in our wrong choices, decisions will become unclear and difficult to control.

Our freedom of choice is tied to our attitudes and daily actions, which, whether good or bad, will have their consequences. If we misuse our bodies, our time on Earth and everything we have at our disposal, this option (*"You decide"*) may not be offered in the final stages of our lives, which we do not know when it will occur.

The option to choose, or "decide" for ourselves was granted to us throughout our existence and yet, we often do not stop to analyze the pros and cons of many of our choices.

If we are not careful now, we will only be left to watch our chances to make better choices run out and our time expires, regardless of our age.

A suggestion:

"May our greatest concerns be centered on not hurting or disappointing our Heavenly Father, Our Creator", this way we will have a greater chance of getting things right.

From the valuable guidance I received:

"- Stay close to the tree!"

According to Revelations 2:7;

"...we will be given to eat of the tree of life, which is in the paradise of God"; or

" the tree of the knowledge of good and evil" as described in Genesis.

Regarding staying close to the tree, which I was instructed to do, it would be an allusion to the "tree of life" which is the representation of God's Love and His Gospel, which produces the sweetest and whitest fruits that exist, from which we can learn to make assertive choices.

From these fruits come peace and true happiness, as recounted in 1 Nephi chapter 8 in the Book of Mormon.

Let us stay close to this "Tree" and not stray, for we will not be safe far from the love and protection of Our Father.

THE END

About the author

R.S. Guidolin graduated in pedagogy in the Oeste Paulista University, Brazil. She was a teacher and then director/owner of Le Savant College. Married to Ozair de Jesus Ribeiro Filho, they built a beautiful family together, with 21 children and 29 grandchildren. She is also the author of the books: "Laços eternos" , "Gório" e "Vinte e Três - Uma família além da conta"

Made in United States
Troutdale, OR
05/16/2025

31413907R00062